I0163789

# The Gospel of Inclusion

# The Gospel of Inclusion

*Exploring Our Divine Family Tree*

*By Wade Galt*

Possibility Infinity Publishing

Copyright © 2007, 2020 by Wade Galt – All Rights Reserved

Published and distributed by:

Possibility Infinity Publishing


No part of this book may be used or reproduced in any manner whatsoever
without written permission from the publisher – other than for "fair use"
as brief quotations embodied in articles, books and reviews.


ISBN  978-1-934108-21-5

# To God...

*Our Father, Our Mother,*
*Our Creator, Our Everything.*

# These Ideas Work For Me...

I wouldn't call them beliefs because I'm not attached to them. I'm not ready to kill or die to prove I'm right or that someone else is wrong. This is not dogma, so there's no need for anyone to argue. I'm not suggesting I'm right or others are wrong. I may be incorrect. I'm not saying I hold the only truth, the ultimate truth, or even truth.

This book is a collection of ideas that feel true to me, that inspire me, and that work for me (based on what I can see in my life). I'd love to hear how these and other ideas work for you. I see this as a two-way learning relationship that we can both learn from. I'm not the teacher. You're not the student. We're just two people exploring ideas about the divine in hope of improving our lives and the world.

## Please Accept My Humility and My Grandiosity

It is my only intention that this work brings you closer to peace, love, joy, happiness, and a greater connection with the divine. Please excuse my limitations as a writer as I attempt to do this. It is not my intention to make anyone feel wrong, uncomfortable, that they need to change, or feel anything other than fully loved, accepted and supported.

Please accept my grandiosity in wanting to address such a huge and important subject (and any apparent presumption that I'm right). Please also accept my humility in doing my best to make myself vulnerable by sharing something I think will make the world a better place. I honor all those people, organizations, religions, beliefs, rituals, and everything else that seeks to do the same,

At the same time, I remain excited, open-hearted and open-minded to seeing how we may grow, evolve, and change how we relate with the divine and each other to bring about even more peace, love, and happiness.

Two children and their parents went to the park to play on the playground.

As soon as they arrived at the park, the older child wanted to leave.

"Not again," the older child complained. "I don't want to play with those kids. They are different from me. They are not as smart as me. They are not as nice as me, and they are not as loveable as me."

"*What do you mean?*" *asked the younger child.*

"*Their skin color is different from mine,*" *said the older child.* "*I don't like them.*"

"My skin is different than yours because I was out in the sun," the younger child replied. "Do you still love me? If you don't, I can stay out of the sun so my skin will become the same as yours again. I just want you to love me."

"Of course I love you," said the older child. "Don't be foolish. We have the same parents. We are from the same family. I will love you no matter how dark or how light your skin becomes."

"Thank you for loving me no matter what color my skin is," replied the younger child. "That means a lot to me. Do you also love our cousins? They have a different skin color than both of us."

"Yes, I love them, too," said the older child. "We have the same grandparents. We are from the same family. I will love them no matter how dark or how light their skin becomes."

"That's great," cheered the younger child. "It's nice to be a part of a loving family."

"Yes, it is," replied the older child.

"Do you love our second cousins, too?" asked the younger child.


"Yes, I love them, too," said the older child. "We have the same great grandparents. We are from the same family."

*"How about our third cousins?" asked the younger child. "Do you love them, as well?"*

*"Yes, I love them, too," said the older child. "We have the same great great grandparents. We are from the same family."*

"What about our tenth cousins and our hundredth cousins?" continued the younger child. "How far does our family reach? When are they no longer our family? When do you stop loving them?"

"I don't know," replied the older child. The older child did not have an answer to that question.

*It bothered the older child to not have an answer to that question. The older child had been very loving towards cousins and second cousins, but was not sure about the other cousins who were further out in the family tree.*

*The younger child became more curious with the answer because it was the first time "I don't know" was an answer from the older child. The younger child wanted to know more.*

*"If I needed money, and you had it,*
*would you give it to me?"*
*asked the younger child.*

*"Of course I would,"*
*replied the older child.*

*"What if I needed clothes or food or a place to live?" asked the younger child.*

*"If I could afford to give it to you, I would," replied the older child. "And if I couldn't afford it, I would do everything I could to be able to afford it."*

*"Wow!" exclaimed the younger child, genuinely surprised. "You would do that for me?"*

*"Without a doubt," replied the older child confidently and proudly.*

*"Why would you do that?"* the younger child begged to know.

*"We are from the same family,"* replied the older child. *"I would do that for all my family members."*

*"That's great,"* replied the younger child in amazement. *"Would you do it for our cousins?"*

*"If I could,"* the older child replied, *"I certainly would."*

"*What about our third and tenth and hundredth cousins?*" the young child asked.

"*I don't know,*" the older child said humbly.

*All the questions bothered the older child. The questions made him examine how he treated others. He thought he always helped his family members, but now he was not so sure who was a part of his family and who was not.*

*The younger child appeared ready to ask another set of questions, but the older child interrupted the younger one. "I think I need to ask Mom and Dad some questions first. I don't know as much as I thought I did."*

*The older child asked his mother,
"Who are my family members?"*

*The mother had overheard the two
children talking. "Who do you
think your family members are?"*

"Well, I know that you and dad are part of my family," the child replied. "And I know my little sister is a part of my family."

"Yes," she replied.
"Is there anyone else?"

*"Then there are my cousins and second cousins," he answered, looking at her to see if she was nodding in agreement to his answer.*

*"Yes," she replied.*

*She paused and waited.*

"*How many cousins do I have?*"

*he asked.*

"*That's a great question,*" *she*
*replied.* "*I'm not sure.*"

*"How far out do I need to go before people stop being my cousins and are no longer part of my family?" he asked.*

*"That's an even better question," she responded.*
*"What do you think?"*

*"I guess it depends on how I define 'family', " he replied.*

*"It seems to me that you are correct," she replied.*

*"So how do you define it?"*

*"I think that my family is everyone who came from the same original parents as I did, no matter how many generations back I go,"* he said, proud of his answer.

"That's a very interesting answer,"
his mother replied.
"So how do you find the beginning
of the family tree?"

"I don't think there are historical
records that go that far back,"
he said.

*"If you went all the way to the beginning of your family tree, where do you think it would start?" she asked.*

*"I guess it would start with God," he replied. "Wouldn't it?"*

*"That is what I think is true,"*

*she replied.*

*"Yes," he confirmed. "That makes sense to me. I feel very confident about that answer."*

*"Do you see that boy on the playground?"* asked the mother.

*"Yes, I do,"* he replied.

*"If you went all the way to the beginning of his family tree, where do you think it would start?"*

*she asked.*

"*I guess it would start with God, too,*" *he replied.* "*Wouldn't it?*"

"*That is what I think is true,*" *she replied.*

*"If that's the case, then it's probably true that everyone's family tree starts with God,"* he concluded.

*"It seems that way to me,"* she agreed.

*"Then are you telling me that everyone is my family member?" he asked.*

*"Actually," she responded, "that is what you are telling me."*

*"But that seems impossible!" he exclaimed. "These people have different skin color than mine."*

*"If I went to an island and got the darkest tan in the world, would that change the fact that I am your mother?"* she asked.

*"No, it wouldn't,"* he conceded.

"And what if your father went and lived in the coldest and darkest part of the world and his skin became pale white," she continued. "Would that stop him from being your father?"

"No, it wouldn't change a thing," he agreed.

*"If your sister moved half way around the world, wore a bone in her nose, worshipped a fire hydrant because she thought it was God, became a thief, painted her skin purple with pink polka dots, shaved her hair, and ate grass,"* the mother continued, *"Would that change the fact that she's your sister?"*

"No, it wouldn't change a thing,"

he admitted.

*"Welcome to the family!"*

*his father shouted.*

*"What do you mean?"*

*the boy asked.*

*"You now have over 7 billion family members living on the planet," the father shared. "You have been living with them all your life, but you have never recognized them."*

*"I see," replied the young boy. "I never thought of it that way."*

*"Do you know who that boy on the playground is?" the father asked.*

*"No," the boy replied. "How am I supposed to know that?"*

*"You don't know who he is?" the father asked again.*

*"No," the boy replied impatiently.*

*"That's our brother," replied the*

*younger sister.*

*"That's right,"* said the father. *"And do you know who that girl on the playground is?"*

*"I get it,"* the boy replied. *"That's my sister."*

*"If you truly understand that," the father shared, "You will always be open to playing with your brothers and sisters on the playground and sharing it with them."*

*"I see," replied the boy.*

*"If you truly see them as your family, then you will treat them like your family and love them like your family," the mother continued.*

*"And many of them will be changed by your example and treat you and love you like their family," agreed the father.*

*"How come all of them don't always treat me like I am part of their family?" the boy asked.*

*"They may not recognize you as part of their family,"*
*the mother answered.*
*"They may not realize it."*

*"Then how should I treat them if they don't treat me like family?"*

*asked the boy.*

*"When your little sister was born, did she seem to know you were part of her family?"* asked the father.

*"I guess not,"* replied the boy.

"*Did that change the fact that she was and is a part of your family?*" the father continued.

"*No,*" the boy replied. "*It didn't.*"

*"So how did you treat her?"*

*asked the father.*

*"I treated her like she was part of*

*my family," the boy answered.*

*"Exactly,"* confirmed the mother.

*"If everyone in the world is a part of my family,"* the boy thought out loud, *"then how do I help take care of my family?"*

"*What exactly do you mean?*" asked the mother. She had an idea what he meant, but she wanted him to process all of it and think it through completely.

"Some of my family members have no food," he observed. "How do I feed them? Some have no home. How do I help them find a place to live? Some of them are lonely. How can I make sure they have friends?"

"Those are great questions," replied the mother.

"You seem to truly care about your family. As you can see, it's not so easy to just watch problems happen in the world when they happen to the ones you love."

*"Even though there is so much food in the world, some of our family members starve,"* added the father. *"Though there is much shelter, many have no home. Even though there are over 7 billion people on the planet, many are lonely."*

*"Why does this happen?"*
asked the boy.

*"Probably because not everyone in the world sees everyone else as their family member,"* the mother answered. *"If they did, they would probably not sit by and watch while their brothers and sisters go without."*

*"It is much easier to see other people as just other random people who are not a part of our family,"* said the father, *"because it makes it possible for us to ignore their problems and still feel comfortable with ourselves."*

*"But isn't it obvious that we're all part of the same family?" asked the son.*

*"It wasn't so obvious to you just a few minutes ago," said the mother. "It isn't so obvious to everyone else."*

*"Can't adults see the truth?"*

*asked the boy.*

*"Aren't most adults taught that we*

*are all God's children?"*

"Many of us are taught that," the mother replied. "But sometimes we believe that only some of us are God's children. Sometimes we tell ourselves that we are special and others are not. Sometimes we even tell ourselves that others are not as good as us or don't deserve as many good things out of life as we do."

"Why do we do that?" the boy replied. "Isn't that selfish?"

His mother answered with a question, "When you don't want to share with your sister, how do you justify it? How do you convince yourself that you deserve something and she doesn't?"

*"I share!" the boy replied*

*defensively.*

*"Do you always share?"*

*asked the father.*

"No," the boy replied. "I share when I think there's enough for everybody, but I don't usually share when I think I might lose something by sharing."

"*Do you remember earlier today when there was one lollipop left, and your sister wanted it?*" asked the mother. The boy nodded. "*What did you tell me when I asked you to allow her to have it?*"

*"I told you that she didn't clean
her room like you told her,
so she didn't deserve it,"
he answered honestly.*

"*Did I ask you to give it to her only if she obeyed me?*"
the mother asked.

"*No,*" he admitted. "*It just seemed like a good way to justify why I should get it and she should not.*"

*"Did you know there was another lollipop in the house?"* she asked. *"And it was your favorite flavor."*

*"I didn't know that,"* replied the boy. *"I would have shared if I knew that. Why didn't you tell me?"*

"*We have always told you that we will do whatever we can to give you what you want and what you need when you want it and when you need it,*" *the father replied.*

"*And we have also told you that God will always make sure you have what you need,*" the mother added. "*If you know that, then you do not need to worry about not having enough. There is always enough.*"

*"But even though there is always enough," replied the boy, "people don't always share. How do I make others share?"*

"People need to decide for themselves if they wish to share. It's very difficult to make people want to share," replied the father. "You can always start by sharing first, though."

*"But what if they don't share back?" asked the boy.*

*"I know you have told me that my needs will still be met, but if people don't share then some people go without food or clothing or shelter or friendship. How do we get others to share?"*

*"There are two answers to that question that I am aware of,"* replied the mother.

*"First, if you share with others, and you know that you will always have enough, you will teach others to share and then they can experience that they have enough. People usually cannot or will not share until they know there is enough for themselves first."*

"That makes sense," replied the boy. "I will do that as much as I can. What's the second answer?"

*"When your sister asked you a question you did not know how to answer, what did you do?"* asked the father.

*"I asked someone who knows more than I do,"* the boy replied.

"*That is what we do, too,*"
replied the father.
"*When we don't know the answer,
we ask God for guidance.*"

"*I see,*" replied the boy.
"*So I should ask God why
people won't share?*"

"You can do that," replied the mother. "One piece of wisdom might help you. It is usually most helpful to ask HOW to fix something rather than WHY it is broken. If you really want to fix it, HOW is critically important, and WHY is less important (other than possibly helping figure out HOW). Very often you don't need the WHY to figure the HOW."

"Yes," agreed the father. "If you listen well, you will notice that people who most want to fix problems ask HOW questions and focus on HOW because they are so committed to fixing the problem. People who want to justify problems, avoid fixing them, or feel too overwhelmed to take action usually ask WHY questions and try to defend WHY they are unable or unwilling to fix the problem."

*"So all I need to do is ask?"*

*asked the boy.*

*His parents nodded.*

*"Just ask your questions and listen," his father replied.*

*"Your questions are very important, but it is even more important that you listen. Go ahead and ask your questions now. And then listen!"*

"Dear God. How can we learn to share? How can we all recognize that we are all one family? How can we come to understand that there is enough for everyone? What can I do to help? How can I make the world a better place? How can I include all the people in my divine family? What can I do at this moment to create harmony and connection in the world?"

*LISTEN...*

# *What I Would Do For My Family*

*I would give the shirt off my back for my brother.*

*I would give my last loaf of bread to my sister.*

*I would give my mother my bed if she had no place to sleep.*

*I would visit my father if he were lonely no matter where he may be.*

*I would do everything in my power to support my family, love my family, and make them feel welcome.*

*Who is my brother?*

*Who is my sister?*

*Who is my mother?*

*Who is my father?*

*Who is my family?*

## Acknowledgments

Thank you God… for including me and all our family in your plan. I know I forget sometimes, and I know I do not always live my life from this place of understanding. I know sometimes I think I am better, more holy, more loving, more deserving, and more a part of your family than others. Thank you for being patient with me and for loving me at every step in the journey.

My intention is that all who read this book, including myself, will experience the joy, bliss and fulfillment that come from knowing that we all are a part of your family – regardless of our beliefs, race, color, gender, orientation, religion or any other variable.

## About the Author

Wade has led retreats and personal growth workshops, authored books on spirituality, personal growth, finance, parenting, business growth & more.

He has worked successfully as a life coach, 4-day work week mentor, organizational consultant, computer trainer, sales consultant, executive coach, speaker, mental health counselor, management consultant, software designer and programmer, author, business analyst, financial counselor, and in many other capacities.

Wade has a Bachelor's degree in Marketing and a Master's degree in Mental Health Counseling Psychology.

He lives happily with his wife, children, and dog.


His email address is wade@wadegalt.com .


## Author Blog & Website

You may visit Wade's blog & website at www.wadegalt.com .


## New Book & Online Course Notifications

If you'd like to be emailed when we release new books, audios and other programs please visit www.wadegalt.com/notify to sign up for these notifications.

# *Also by Wade Galt*

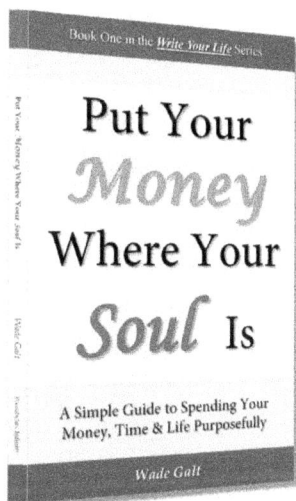

**Put Your Money Where Your Soul Is**

A Simple Guide to Spending Your
Money, Time and Life Purposefully

*Learn how to free up additional time,
money and energy by redefining your
relationships with money, time, people,
and things.*

*Simple strategies, exercises & tools help
you make powerful changes with very
little effort or struggle.*

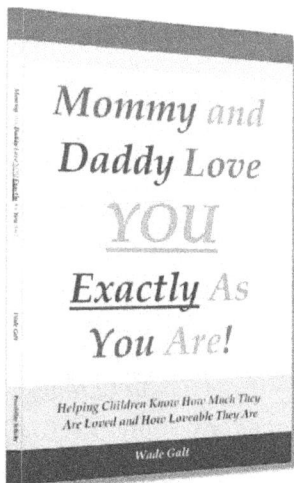

**Mommy and Daddy Love You
Exactly As You Are!**

Helping Children Know How Much They
Are Loved and How Loveable They Are

*My hope is that this book helps you...*

*1) Let your child or children know how
special they are.*

*2) Remember how special your child or
children are.*

*3) Understand how much your parents
love(d) you, whether or not they ever
shared this with you.*

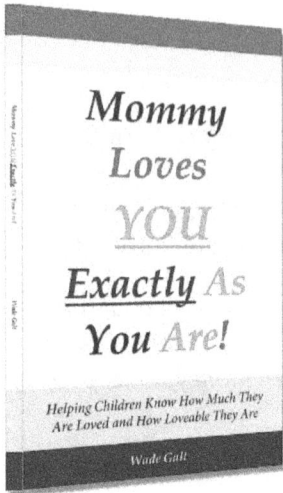

## Mommy Loves You Exactly As You Are!

Helping Children Know How Much They Are Loved and How Loveable They Are

*My hope is that this book helps you...*

*1) Let your child or children know how special they are.*

*2) Remember how special your child or children are.*

*3) Understand how much your parents love(d) you, whether or not they ever shared this with you.*

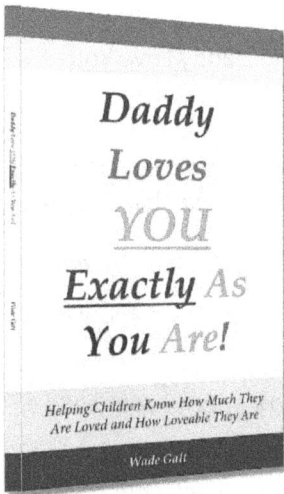

## Daddy Loves You Exactly As You Are!

Helping Children Know How Much They Are Loved and How Loveable They Are

*My hope is that this book helps you...*

*1) Let your child or children know how special they are.*

*2) Remember how special your child or children are.*

*3) Understand how much your parents love(d) you, whether or not they ever shared this with you.*

# The *God Equals Love* Book Series

(Free eBook Versions Available for All Books)

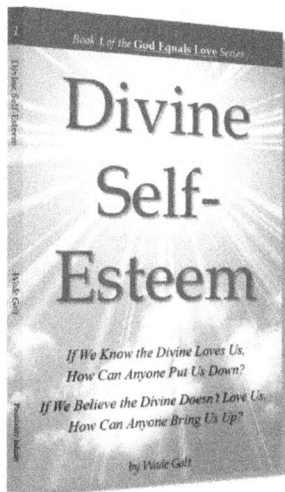

<u>Book 1 - Divine Self-Esteem</u>

Learning to Love Ourselves
the Way the Divine Loves Us

*If we know the Divine loves us, how can anyone put us down?*

*If we believe the Divine doesn't love us, how can anyone bring us up?*

*Learn to see yourself through divinely loving eyes and catch a glimpse of the divinely-made miracle you are.*

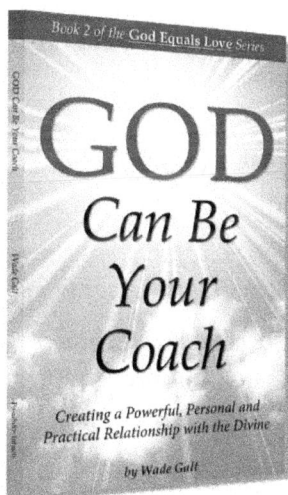

<u>Book 2 - GOD Can Be Your Coach</u>

Creating a Powerful, Personal and
Practical Relationship with the Divine

*Create More Joy, Happiness, Love, Peace and Purpose in Your Life.*

*Learn One Simple Way to form a more powerful connection & relationship.*

*If You Knew You Could Connect with the Divine Anytime You Choose to Receive Guidance, Support, and Peace, Would You?*

*Will You?*

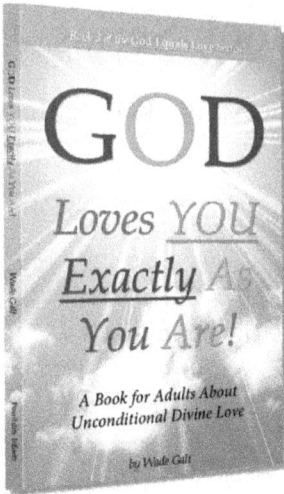

### 3 - GOD Loves You Exactly As You Are!

#### Understanding & Experiencing Unconditional Divine Love

*An Invitation to Consider & Experience the Life-Altering Understanding That You are Completely and Unconditionally Loved and Loveable EXACTLY AS YOU ARE!*

*What If God Loves You EXACTLY as You are?*

*How Would Understanding that Transform Your Life?*

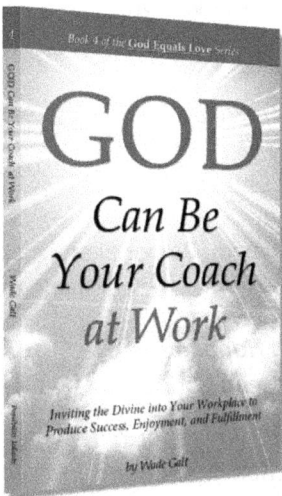

### Book 4 - GOD Can Be Your Coach at Work

Inviting the Divine into Your Workplace to Produce Success, Enjoyment & Fulfillment

*Few of us fully live our highest spiritual values in our workplace.*

*This is a source of frustration, shame, guilt & dissatisfaction for billions of us.*

*What if the divine actually wants us to experience life, love, joy, fulfillment, and abundance inside and outside our work?*

*What if the divine cares about our work simply because the divine cares for us?*

*This book is an invitation to work WITH the divine to create divinely inspired results for you and the world.*

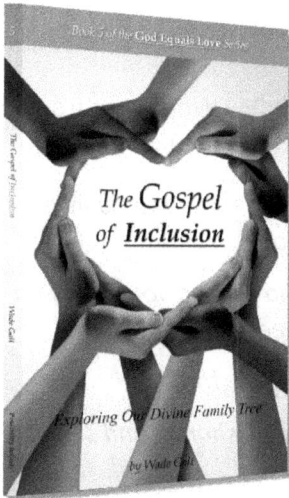

## Book 5 - The Gospel of Inclusion

### Exploring Our Divine Family Tree

*Who is included in God's plan? Is it only people like me? Only people like you? What atrocities & apathy do we justify daily by declaring others are outside of God's chosen circle of people?*

*What if we really are part of one divine family? What would that mean? How would we have to change?*

*WARNING! Reading this book may lead you to (1) consider the possibility that we're all God's children and (2) do something about that. Proceed at your own risk!*

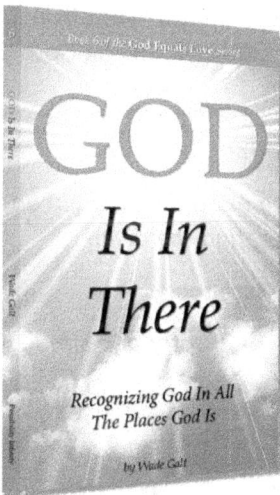

## Book 6 - God Is In There

### Recognizing God In All The Places God Is

*If you could teach only one spiritual lesson, what would you teach?*

*What truth could you share that is so powerful, it would fundamentally transform the way others live?*

*There are a few core ideas that most spiritual traditions hold as true. Some believe that the most powerful and life-transforming truths are so self-evident and so obvious that all traditions agree about them.*

*This book contains one of those ideas.*

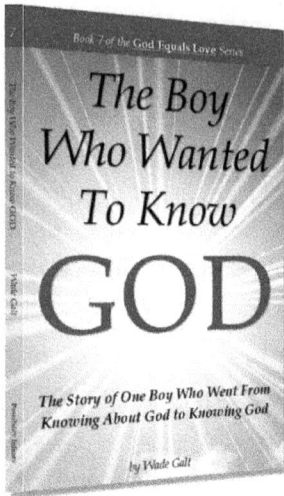

### 7 - The Boy Who Wanted to Know God

The Story of One Boy Who Went from Knowing About God to Knowing God

*What would you be willing to do in order to meet God?*

*Join a curious and excited young boy on his journey to meeting the divine.*

*You might meet God, too.*

*The journey may be shorter and simpler than you think.*

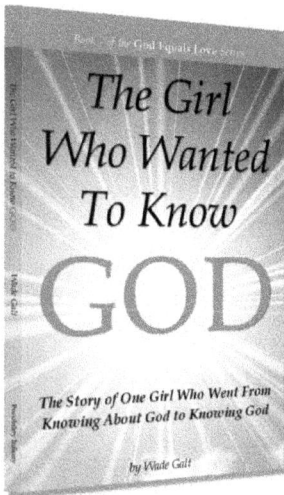

### 7 - The Girl Who Wanted to Know God

The Story of One Girl Who Went from Knowing About God to Knowing God

*What would you be willing to do in order to meet God?*

*Join a curious and excited young girl on her journey to meeting the divine.*

*You might meet God, too.*

*The journey may be shorter and simpler than you think.*

# *Translated into Spanish* (More to Come)

## Autoestima Divina

Aprendiendo a Amarnos De la
Forma en que Dios nos Ama

*Si sabemos que el Divino nos ama,
¿cómo podemos sentirnos mal con
nosotros mismos?*

*Si creemos que el Divino no nos ama,
¿cómo podemos sentirnos bien con
nosotros mismos?*

*Aprender a verse a sí mismo a través de
los ojos de amor de Dios y echar un
vistazo a el milagro hecho de Dios-que
eres.*

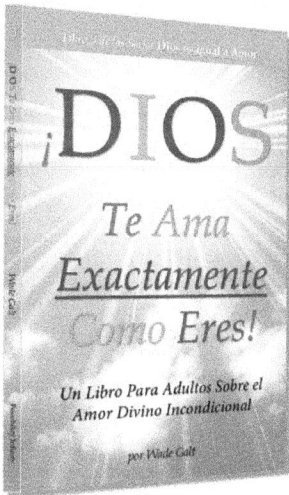

## DIOS Te Ama Exactamente Como Eres

Un Libro Para Adultos Sobre el Amor
Divino Incondicional

*¿Y Si Dios te ama EXACTAMENTE como
eres? ¿De que manera ese entendimiento
transformaría tu vida?*

*Esto Es Una Simple Invitación... Para
Considerar y Experimentar... Un
Entendimiento de la Vida Alternativo...*

*Tú Eres Completa e Incondicionalmente...
Amado y Adorable... EXACTAMENTE
COMO ERES!*

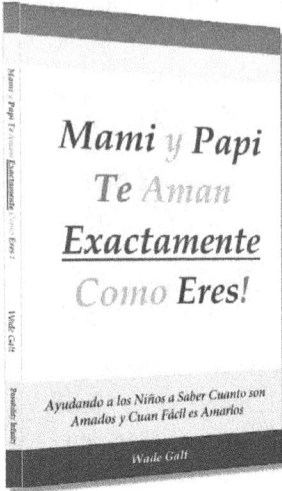

## Mami y Papi Te Aman Exactamente Como Eres!

Ayudando a los Niños a Saber Cuanto son Amados y Cuan Fácil es Amarlos

*Mi esperanza es que este libro te ayude a...*

*1) Hacer que tus niños sepan cuan especiales son.*

*2) Recordarte cuan especiales son tus niños.*

*3) Comprender cuanto te aman o te amaron tus padres ya sea que compartieran o no esto contigo.*

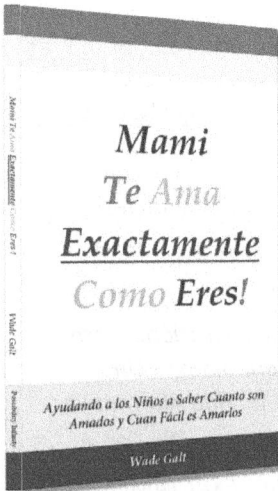


## Mami Te Ama Exactamente Como Eres!

Ayudando a los Niños a Saber Cuanto son Amados y Cuan Fácil es Amarlos

*Mi esperanza es que este libro te ayude a...*

*1) Hacer que tus niños sepan cuan especiales son.*

*2) Recordarte cuan especiales son tus niños.*

*3) Comprender cuanto te aman o te amaron tus padres ya sea que compartieran o no esto contigo.*

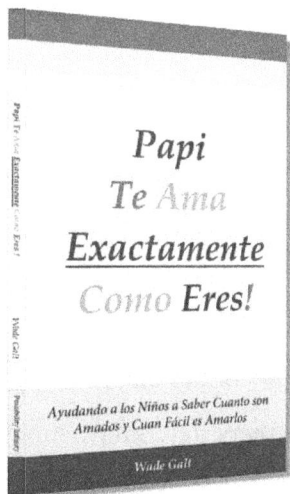

## Papi Te Ama Exactamente Como Eres!

Ayudando a los Niños a Saber Cuanto son Amados y Cuan Fácil es Amarlos

*Mi esperanza es que este libro te ayude a...*

*1) Hacer que tus niños sepan cuan especiales son.*

*2) Recordarte cuan especiales son tus niños.*

*3) Comprender cuanto te aman o te amaron tus padres ya sea que compartieran o no esto contigo.*

To see these books and other books not listed here, visit www.wadegalt.com/books .

All profits from the sale of the GOD EQUALS LOVE books go to organizations and charities that seek to end unnecessary hunger and poverty.

# Share the Message & the Love

I hope this helps you see & feel how connected we all are in our Divine Family Tree and inspires you to share and enjoy that connection with your fellow family members.

If you found the book to be helpful, would you please be so kind as to write a review for the book or share the book on Facebook, Instagram, Twitter or other social media so others may know how it helped you?

Even if it's a super-short review, every little bit helps.

Thank you so much.

If there's anything I can do to help you further with this work, please email me at is wade@wadegalt.com .

All my best,

Wade

www.ingramcontent.com/pod-product-compliance
Lightning Source LLC
Chambersburg PA
CBHW070641030426
42337CB00020B/4113

* 9 7 8 1 9 3 4 1 0 8 2 1 5 *